The Dark Side of My Mind

Volume 8

Briana Blair

The Dark Side of My Mind Volume 8

Copyright © 2010, Briana Blair

ISBN 978-0-557-76143-2

All rights reserved by the author. No part of this publication can be reproduced, stored in a retrieval system, or transmitted in any form or by any means, electronic, mechanical, photocopying, recording or otherwise, without the prior permission of the publishers and/or authors.

Contact me: webmaster@bluedragoncreations.com

Visit my website: http://bluedragoncreations.com/gallery/

Table of Contents

Volume 8

Poems 281 - 320

Come Out - May 1998

Come out, come out

From the place where you hide

The shadows you call protection

Are really bars on your cage

Let's turn another page

And come on out into the light

I know it hurts at first

But not forever

Don't look into the sun

But feel the warmth

The shadows left you cold

And feeling old

So please come out

Let your skin feel

And your eyes see

Come out, come out

And join us in the world

The End - June 1998

My sweet

How you touched me with love

Love not in your nature

A heart so true inside a beast

And to you, I gave

But what I have given, has taken away

And the beast in you returned

And I came to hate That which I had loved

Then there we were

On the verge of the end of the world

I was ready to remove the beast

Then the cursed light returned to your eyes

And my heart was torn

Hate faded with memories of love

A love not meant to be

And so I took you from the world

With a sweet kiss and a steel blade

And all my tears cannot drown this sorrow

The world will live on

But my heart is darkened and dead

And so I leave this place

And all that I have known

This may well have been

The end

Exodus - July 1998

We are all leaving this place

We will all break from the shackles

That have held us back for so long

We will not be

Like our mothers and fathers before us

We will become a new people

Our shared vision will lead us on

The place we have left is a racist world

The shackles that bound us were our bigotry

We will change the beliefs of the new generation

Our common goal is peace and unity

And if we travel together

We will find a way

Paradise Dream - July 1998

I close my eyes

And the night is a passage

To a place beyond

And here my dreams

Are my reality

Here I can be who I choose to be

I can be strong and wild and courageous

The weakness and pain

Of the waking world

Cannot hold me down here

And these dreams

Take me from my hell

And into paradise

A paradise from which

I wish I would not wake

Expressions - July 1998

These words come walking

Creeping, seeping

Dripping out of cracks and spaces

Filling up the empty places

Searching, seeking

Finding truth

Seeing the future

Remembering youth

The words come sneaking

Crawling, sprawling

Always out there

I hear them calling

The words are mine

The words are free

They're always, always

Here in me

Feels Like Home - August 1998

She sits alone

In an abysmal darkness

Surrounded by claustrophobic walls

And there is a silence

Almost deafening

She has traveled through a maze

Of pains and sorrows

And that path has led her here

Here to this place of emptiness

It almost feels like home

Dark Retreat - September 1998

The darkness

Is peaceful

My escape

My sanctuary

The darkness

Once a frightening place

Of fear and nightmares

Now my only retreat

From the tortures of day

And though my nights are sleepless

The darkness brings me comfort

For the shadows hide

The things I fear

And here I wish to stay

Rivers to Oceans - September 1998

Sometimes

I want to cry

To shed tears that make a river

A river that makes an ocean

For there is pain inside me

Pain that no one understands

My life is constant torment

My eyes are clouds of constant rain

And no one comprehends

The battles in my mind

The aching in my heart

The salvation I can't find

And so I cry my river

And so it makes my ocean

And though inside I'm dying

Somehow my life goes on

Winter Of The Heart - October 1998

I am cold

I touch my hand

Upon the flame

And embrace its fiery burn

But it does not warm my soul

That part is so unreachable

Untouchable by flame

Encased in fear and sorrow

My heart is the home of despair

My eyes the windows of agony

My lips the doors to anger

They dwell in me

As I dwell in nothingness

Ever-growing coldness

It is forever winter

In my heart

Inseparable - October 1998

The blackness

It speaks volumes

Inaudible thoughts

Scream to me

Piercing me

Cutting deeply

Scarring the very heart of me

But pain no longer comforts me

There is only empty numbness

An unfathomable coldness

Something so deep

So deep it's inconceivable

But it...

Is

It exists

It grasps

And tears

And penetrates

And how I crave to carve it out

But we are one

And so... Inseparable

Fear's Shadows - January 1999

There.

I see it.

A bare variance from the darkness…

But it is there…

A shadow among shadows.

It cringes in a corner

Stealing away in the blackness

Unknown to any…

Any but me…

Yes, I know this one

This one

My companion

My enemy

My fear

And he lurks there in the ebony places of my soul

Waiting

For a moment when he may strike me down

But I shall fight this cowering beast

I will do my best to lighten his shadows

I will not be taken by this one…

Not yet

The Beast Within - January 1999

There is no beast

Like the beast within

No terror as frightening

As the truth of one's own soul

Nothing can strike terror

The way the mirror can

To reflect upon one's self

Is often to look into the face of hell

But fear not the evil within

Fight

And never give in

Weary Soul - January 1999

How many tears can be shed by one's eyes?

How much heartache can one soul endure?

How much can one heart pay

When it has committed no crime?

I do not know, but I fear I will

The world is cruel

And strife is laden upon the good

While wealth upon the evil

It is hard to say

How long one can go without hope

Time seems eternity without happiness

Days seem dark without prospect

But there is no respite for a weary soul

It must go on

Even when it is unsure of just how

My Crime - January 1999

Blackened heart

Burned soul

Charred remains

Of life's goal

Reddened eyes

And blue tears

No reward

For painful years

Shadowed nights

And days of grey

For what crime

Is it I pay?

More Than Being - January 1999

I feel so empty…

The wells of my tears have run dry

My soul and heart

Are but sandy deserts

Barren and lonely

My heart aches

And my mind reels

But there is no comfort

No release

Almost nothing at all

I fear that all life's pains

Have made me grow cold

There are no highs or lows

Just being

Just a terrible, lonely emptiness

And longing

What I would give for the power to scream

To cry, to feel

To know I'm more than just here

To know that I'm still alive

Loathing - August 1999

Loathing

Is what I feel for you

Hate and disgust

You inspire, it's true

I once thought you were wonderful

Held you close to my heart

Now I despise the thought of you

And want to rip yours apart

You are the lowest of all the things I know

Evil, and full of deceit

Even the devil would bow to you

I know he can't compete

I can't believe I loved you

Gave you my heart and soul

Now I believe that to scare and hurt me

Has always been your goal

But someday you'll regret

When at last I get away

For you'll be all alone

Until your dying day

Song Of The Bell - October 1999

No more heartache shall I feel

When his memory comes to mind

I shall know my inner strength

Peace and hope I'll find

Not another tear be shed

No more pain inside my head

I'll be at peace with his memory

And he will be at peace with me

As my heart heals, so his shall too

With hearts at ease, we'll see life anew

No more tears or sorrowed dreams

Now we'll see jus what life means

My soul at peace and his as well

So shall it be, when I ring this bell

Passion - October 1999

I wish to drink, But there is no water

I wish to breathe, But there is no air

I yearn to touch, But there is no one

I am cold and lonely and bare

I look for comfort, But there is sorrow

I look for love, But there is pain

I walk on paths, But they are mountains

I reach for sunshine, But there is rain

And what does yearning do

But cause the soul to ache

And what does wanting do

But cause your heart to break

Why is it human souls desire

Why is there this

Burning fire

I know not

But it is

It is in and on and about and through

It is all and nothing, And everything

It is this that drives us

It is this that makes us

Whole

Complete

And yet ever-yearning

Secret Shadows - *June 2001*

Here we are

In our secret shadows

The faint moon-glow in our eyes

The air whispers with the sounds of nature

And beats with the rhythm of our hearts

I see your face

Your shy, sweet smile

And feel as though I could melt into your arms

And I know we feel the same

And then it happens…

The soft, gentle touch

And the sweet warmth of your lips on mine

I feel our hearts race together

In a moment we wish could last forever

Seed of Love - July 2001

We have planted a seed of love

And willed it to grow in the garden of hope

And here there is no room for doubt

For doubt is the seed of death

Its roots will strangle love

Its blooms will spore fear and hate

They will grow firm and steal love's light

But there is no doubt planted here

We grow faith and trust beside our love

They will grow strong and reach for the light

Like them we will grow together

We will bend with the winds of change and not break

We will draw strength from The Mother

And bask in the warmth of The Father

And they will help us to stand the test of time.

Buried - October 2001

I am here

Buried beneath your neglect

Like some World Trade Center victim

Gasping for breath beneath the rubble

The dust of your heartlessness

Choking my lungs

Will you find me?

Will you come to search me out

And save my heart?

Or will you leave me here

My broken walls pushing down on me

Crushing me

Will you defuse the time bomb

You left ticking in my heart

Or is it already too late?

Reality - January 2003

When you think, What you feel

When you give, What you steal

Then you'll see what is real

This is your reality

Live for what you feel

Live your life

Make it real

Only speak, What you know

Take the ride, Let it flow

Take it in

Them let it go

Then it becomes

Reality

It becomes reality

Live for what you feel

Live your life

Make it real

Don't let denial

Be confusion

Time is just

An illusion

It's just

Your mind's pollution

Don't deny reality

The Way - ? 2006

That light-heavy feeling

Tied down and spinning

Lead weights wrapped in cotton

Sharp pain and cloudy mind

Fast determination coiled in doubt

Wanting, needing

Fearing, fleeing

Deep inside myself

Clawing, crying to get out

Weeping, begging to stay in

Wanting, needing

To shed the searing numbness

To have, to be, to know

To grasp the elusive clarity

And find the way

The Angel Comes - ? 2006

The sound of wings Beating on the wind

A thing of awe and beauty

But she is not the stuff of dreams

No white wings or golden curls

She is black fury Flying through the night

Cutting through the sky

Like cold razors through flesh

She brings the word of doom

The promise of oblivion

And I go to her

Wrap myself in her ebony embrace

Feel the chill of time and fear

Flow through her

And into me

I revel in the blissful predictability of pain

The comfortable constant

That which never changes

I look into her smiling eyes

See her pleasure in my understanding

For the pain is my passion

My fire and my strength

It is the force that drives me on to another day

And in my weakness she reminds me

Of the power in the darkness of an angel

I Do Not Need This - ? 2006

Cold

The pitch blackness Of your soul

Is like an iceberg

Solid and frozen

Impenetrable

Your selfishness

Like a wall

Like a bridge

Dividing me from you

And you don't care

Your heart is like a brick

Solid and hard

Dead and cold

My hate

Is like a fire

Hot and fierce

Burning and churning

You cannot imagine

But if you please

If you try

You can make me cry

You can make me bleed

And make me cold

I do not need this from you

I'll Go - ? 2006

I am alive

But I wish I'd died

Long ago

I do not know

Why my love's in vain

Why I feel this pain

I give to you

My heart was true

My heart's my vice

You are like ice

There is no use

It's just misuse

Mistrust and hate

I close the gate

And close my heart

I must depart

From these ways

And my mind strays

I go away

I cannot stay

With you…

No…

I'll go…

What else can I do?

Shut up Girl (Song Lyrics) - ? 2006

Shut up girl

You know they don't wanna hear you cryin'

Shut up girl

You know they don't care if you're dyin'

Shut up girl

Don't you know everything you say is wrong

Shut up girl

You know the days ain't really that long

No no

Hold on girl

'Cause the world don't owe you a thing

Hold on girl

I know the boy didn't give you that ring

Hold on girl

Even though you think you've had enough

Hold on girl

You know you gotta stand and be tough

Na na na na na na

Yeeaah

Na na na na na

Death, Wait for Me - February 2009

Since I could not wait for Death

I bade death wait for me

To hold the carriage of remorse

Then let it carry me

Unto a place afar from pain

And closer yet to peace

That I might find a way from here

And on to sweet release

The blackness of his eyes was cold

And in them now I knew

My days of woe and ache were gone

My days on Earth were through

His nightmare horses lead us on

Through the forest of regret

And when we reached the Hall of Dark

My final end I met

Death led me from our carriage

And gave me one sweet kiss

Then whispered unto dying ears

There's no sweeter end than this

***Bubble** - February 2010*

Colors

Swirling

Turning

Filmy bubble skin brightness

Churning

Blending

Becoming one

Beautiful

Slick mingling

Becoming one

Pop!

Let's do that again

Don't Cry to Me - February 2010

Frankly dear

I don't give a damn

You don't like me

Waah!

Cry to someone else

Stop it

I'm not rude

I'm just honest

Not my fault you can't take it

This is me

Love it or leave it

I am bold

Beautiful

Independent

And here to stay

Word Zombies - February 2010

I dug my inspiration

Back out of its grave

And it is beautiful!

Slick darkness

Bloody brightness

My muse in all its glory

I am a Goddess

I've revived the dead

The words have risen

Like obedient zombies

Ready to do my bidding

get to work little ones...

The Dark Mistress

Is BACK!

***Inside My Mind* - September 2010**

You think you really know me, don't you?

Trust me, you don't really want to.

But come inside my parlour dear

See all the evil gathered here.

Take a look inside my mind

Oh what horrors you will find.

Beasties built of pain and strife

Touch them, watch them come to life.

Don't you like them? Are you scared?

I told you that you weren't prepared.

get out now while you still can

To your shiny waking land.

I told you that you wouldn't like this

But wait, let me give you one kiss.

Take with you a piece of me

From this gift you can't break free.

A gnawing, gripping piece of black

Please do enjoy, and don't come back.

Mental Chains - *September 2010*

Ah, but you hold me down

Mental chains bound tight

Clinging, digging

Pressing into tender places

Breaking will

And crushing spirit

Tearing hope

And bruising dreams

I screamed

My terror filling the air

as you sought to end me

But I prevailed

As I saw that it was you

Who were truly in chains

And I broke free

You couldn't kill me

You just made me stronger

And your chains

Hold me down no more

***Dead Angel* - September 2010**

Come to me my child

My dark, dead angel

Show me the wonders inside your head

Show me the pain

The hate

The death

Let me feel your joy

Your youthful evil wonder

Let us run through the graveyard

Let us torture lost souls

Let us howl at the moon

And revel in the hellish horror

For our time to run is short

Alas, we cannot play forever

The Goddess I Am - October 2010

I am God

I

The fighter

The survivor

I am divinity

I am the power

And the wisdom

I am deserving of worship

I am capable of greatness

I create my own bliss

I need not bow to anyone

I am a Goddess

A light

And through faith in myself

I will shine

How Dare You - October 2010

Hate me

Hurt me

Fucking bitch

Weak, useless shit

Yeah

Tear me down

Beat me

Scare me

Shit on me some more

It's all you know

Pathetic cunt

I'd love to kill you

Rip your eyes out

And watch you bleed

Oh, I remember

Even now

You deserve hell

I hope you fucking bleed

How dare you hurt a child

What A Night - **October 2010**

Suck

Fuck

Love me

Hate me

Tie me up

I'm proud

I'm ashamed

I want

And I fear

What am I?

Who am I?

Take me

Shake me

Thrill me

Kill me

It's all good

Love you

Hate you

Want you

Want truth

What a fucked up night

DeathLoveHatePain - October 2010

DeathLoveHatePain

Love it

Hate it

Wanna be part of it

Yeah I'm a sick fuck

What of it bitch?

You're pathetic

And weak

You hate me

'Cause I embrace this

I love being a freak

I find power in my pain

I know I'm a Goddess

I'm tapping in

Getting closer

You can't fucking touch this

I am heaven

And hell

The It, the Id, the fucking source

And you so wish you could be me

My Goddess - October 2010

Desperation

Motivation

I'm getting so close

I'm tapping in

I thought I'd lost it

But maybe I found it

Son of a bitch

I'm getting it back

My muse

My power

Hell yeah

Incorporating past and present

It's confusing

Sorry if I'm losing you

But it makes perfect sense to me

She heard me calling

No longer falling

My Goddess answered me

Words Return - ***October 2010***

Liquor

Quicker

Thoughts thicker

Honey

Dripping

Sticky sticking

Words

Flowing

Strange Knowing

Words

Return

Lovely Burn

Mine

Again

From Now

'Til When?

www.ingramcontent.com/pod-product-compliance
Ingram Content Group UK Ltd.
Pitfield, Milton Keynes, MK11 3LW, UK
UKHW051134260726
13967UKWH00010B/3042